Working the System
By: Dr. Federica Robinson-Bryant

Working the System by Federica Robinson-Bryant

Published by Denotion Research Group
www.DenotionResearch.com

Cover & Illustrations by TullipStudio

ISBN: 978-1-958634-14-1 (print)

Printed in United States
1st Edition

This book is dedicated to my overly supportive parents. Rest in peace, Daddy!

When I was your age, I liked trying new things, often excited, but sometimes not so much. I typically found value in experiencing something different, and sought opportunities to grow, rather than wishing for luck.

One time I worked at one of the largest defense contractors, supporting a program to refurbish helicopters.

As technology evolved and new standards emerged, those cockpits became the new technology's early adopters. MODERNIZATION they called it.

6

At the government, we had lots of projects- from backpacks and jumbo lasers, to radars and big trucks.

We worked with different teams within and outside our organization to realize new systems and retire others when their time was up. OBSOLETE they would call those.

What can you do in the role of systems engineering? The real question is, "What would you like to do"?

Because the only real boundaries that exist in this field, are those created by you.

16

Can you direct a top secret, artificial intelligence project?
Yes indeed, that's working the system!

20

Can you architect a hands-free gaming console's debut?

Yes indeed, that's working the system!